# Below This Level

# Kelvin Corcoran

# BELOW THIS LEVEL

Shearsman Books

First published in the United Kingdom in 2019 by
Shearsman Books
50 Westons Hill Drive
Emersons Green
BRISTOL
BS16 7DF

Shearsman Books Ltd Registered Office
30–31 St. James Place, Mangotsfield, Bristol BS16 9JB
*(this address not for correspondence)*

www.shearsman.com

ISBN 978-1-84861-684-4

# Diagnosis

## What the Birds Said

I sit by the window and read the poetry received.
I can smell smoke from a neighbour's garden,
hear a collared dove coo, a buried piano, a distant aircraft.
I can understand these things but in my reading
I lose track of the world in the would-be samizdat.

I'm sorry I can't say anything to the generous poet
I'm sorry light is draining from the sky,
that affective meaning has gone in darkness.
This is not a manifesto but longing for first inscription,
to run through the mortal trees with the fox and the rook.

To be saved by names on Rue des Hiboux and Zaventem
I run walk run over bars of light, snow is forecast,
a return to first things is forecast – I like that, said the rook,
I can pick at that, I might eat it and then take off into the sky.

# Run Walk Run

Again I'm off in the morning down the track
stepping through the one-time bars of light with David Bowie;
I swing swing on the monkey bars and pull faces at the cemetery,
suspended above the tilting ground in diagnostic limbo.

Come out come out companions mine,
where are we now and do you have a word to say?
I saw a woman with a three-legged dog
and various corvids posing for Bruegel.

Here's a dawn song for Magnetic Resonance Imaging,
singing inside the tunnel of exploding stars
to make a dark picture from sound I don't want to see;
companions come out and fall come fall gentle rain.

\*

Localised but not metastasised.

We will use all three approaches.

Surgery.  Radiography. Hormone treatment.

Localised not metastasised.

Repeat after me.

No metastasis.  No katabasis.

\*

The track the trees run run walk
could be Spring that dampness
behind me the streets are clear
beggars in place, kids away to school.

This morning's text is from the Reverend Arthur Russell,
'Show me what the girl does to the boy, if you can get around to it.'

I'd say, don't wait around too long for the demo,
I'd say Melanie I remember you, dark girl in the high flat under
      the eaves,
the city a map of lights looking like the whole world spread out
      below us.
Over your shoulder you said, I need this, you said.

I'm down the sunken path with no understanding,
the dark passage of incomprehensible chemistry
and it could be almost greening Spring out there;
bring out the day, let me go.

\*


This morning's darling chorus
a compilation of Glenn Gould's background humming,
his transponder signals from the Bachosphere
as if there are bearings to be found up there.

From which we can reconstruct the music,
the miracle pouring from his fingers
like the flightpaths of the plural world
ascending into depthless blue.

Over the white track through frosted grass
the flights arrive, wheels down, insignia on show,

sliding along a silver cord from everywhere,
easy on the pedals for that music, said Captain Glenn.

\*

Avenue Reine Astrid, Kraainem is a long road
longer than a solo by Neil Young,
with Spring tipping over the Lego houses
and the sun warm enough to tempt the birds to sing.

It's a road as long as hope passing Rue des Tulipes,
keep to the path, don't cross against the lights,
walk boy, talk to Doctor Agneessens, weigh the odds,
carry them through the flatlands in early Spring.

\*

Rain everywhere a thousand mirrors this morning
and with 18 musicians it's crowded on the track,
we bump along as best we can.

A cello rests for breath in the fork of a tree,
comes back in and we're off for Steve Reich racing
over dark holes in the path showing nothing.

Through the trees of the cemetery, a stage set of skips
yellow on red Soret Soret, for the disposal of symbolism;
Oh Soret, little lost thing in the trees, pick up the pace.

\*

In the cool morning my neighbours walk their dogs,
mist pools around their revolving feet hiding the circuit;
*Below this level there is none, the operator said*
and Malcolm Mooney returned to sing the sun up.

I hang from the bar count 90 drop and turn
see the tunnel of light through the swaying trees;
below this level forget the poor soil, the lactic acid burn,
89 90 push the day uphill against katabasis.

*

I walked 100 houses and a fallow field
last lap step-by-step to Centre Medik
to catch corvids blown like rags.

Scant pickings birds, time waits
at the near boundary in falling light,
face like pedantic death.

# The White Road

If I went back there would I hear her voice
and see those figures again, that side of the family
the other side of time folded in the blue and green hills
of the Slad Valley as evening falls under luminous distance
and they work out their lives, come and go,
turn that field to better use, raise children, stop?

There's a patch of light in the sky seems to pause
and shed a painterly quality on common nativity
picturing the practical, hard-bitten characters,
raising the fallen as if still walking long-legged
over hedges, brimming ditches, taking the road to town
with the blue green valley at their backs alight.
I see them come tramping over the fields,
catch the rough old songs beating in their hearts.

\*

The boy dreamt of a white road,
night was all around but the white road shone;
he walked along it thinking it was death
and everything said – no invention is allowed.

Poetry was buried in the mud and muck of the ditch,
he forgot its sound and wondered if it ever happened;
the black trees bore the names of the all the girls he'd known
and the spaces between the things making sense enlarged.

I would rather walk in the Atlantic light of Penwith,
the tilting perspective painted by Ben Nicholson
spilling us east and west into the slapping sea
as we teeter on Celtic fields, skate on granite hedges.

Day recalls that village to the left of the lane,
a bridge of sorts over the pell-mell stream and its aria.

\*

In Europe now, in our city garden,
bats jinx the trees as the light goes
and we sit and talk and talk;
here you are, bright one in darkness.
I can lay out memories like a dance
the days the girls were born
you standing there in a lit doorway
and we walked into a new world.

The silver flightpaths flash above us,
arrival departure, arrival departure;
at the end of the garden is the unknown
and there's no talking there;
only chemistry counts, words fail
walking the damp steps underground.

## Let's Leave

Captain of the turning sea,
do you know the sound a boat makes
hauled up a shingle beach,
do you count through white noise breakers?

I would swim the Picasso Sea,
swim with the women, fish and goats,
ride the bull dripping on the shore
to Paris, Madrid, Barcelona, Antibes.

# Treatment

# Surgery

Wheeled clueless down the white track,
time made absent, memory removed
by the kind surgeon.

*It went well, but I had to take more*
*when I saw inside I knew,*
*it went well but more than planned.*

Five incisions across the abdomen
for robotics and this for extraction,
it went well I hear through fog.

\*

To return awake in the white room,
to see a block of window daylight
and listen to Sibelius
for the world to return over fields of snow,
a country risen in the air-bright score.

My conversation is with nurses
at 3 and 4 in the morning
from Romania, DRC, France and Holland.
My conversation is with the wall
awake all night the wall answers.

— *Thank you, you are very kind.*
— *Oh, it's my job.*
— *It's a very good job, I'm grateful.*
— *You're welcome, it's what I do.*

# Oitgang, provisional

From the bedside by love's hand
the removal of clothes,
the removal of hair,
the removal of thought.

To surrender the beloved
to the care of bright strangers,
to render the body abstract
a creature of biometrics.

*


There but not, afloat like a baby
held in a net of catheters and lines,
dreaming a sky of sensors
in the constellation of data.

Poor Baby Blue in no space no time
hauled back shed a galaxy of blood.
Shovelled into a trench, worked on.
Vision dissolved in black holes.

Nine bright strangers fill the room;
the fabric of thought disintegrates,
a torn cloth stretched and discarded.
Nine bright strangers fill the room.

Voices call then stop and walk away.
What there is of you, next to nothing,
is entirely in the hands of others.
And I hear one voice – Melanie.

*

'The path is through perplexing ways, and when
The goal is gained, we die you know – and then?

What then? I do not know, no more do you,
And so good night.'

\*

Two older nurses work the nightshift,
kind and capable, coaxing in their Flemish.
I think they are familiar, universal aunties.

— *Oh yah we are from the same village,*
— *we have our own language*
— *you have been a good boy, see the numbers.*

I heard them singing in the night
on kitchen chairs in the hospital garden,
taking a break and singing.

— *Oh no, you wouldn't want our singing.*
Of course there is no garden,
and there is a garden where apophenia blooms.

# Radiotherapy

Every day we file under Leopold's triumphal arch
and the river of traffic lands me flat on the radiation table.
— *Bonjour monsieur, ça va? Come down a little, feet in there.*
*No need to help* – a hand on my hip exactly as before.
*We leave you now* – and the monobeat pop music persists.

Clouds drift to the east behind two tower cranes,
over the stripped trees and circuit of roads – *I love love love you.*
I think a city stands and corvids wing me to their plan,
if I hold my arms like this and stand like this, will I fly?
Melanie I didn't mean to lead you to this dry cave.

The satellite panels revolve, the red beams hum as before;
in space my eyes close, count parachute flares in the dark,
the drenched fox stares straight back from the drowned garden,
deep deep bioluminescent forms blossom.
Is there life on Mars? the radio asks.

# Good Science

At night in the courtyard lost in irregular perspective
the dead gather for me and I know them all,
an apple tree rises in bright light, white blossom floods the scene
and my mother as a girl, laughs, reaches up to catch her brother.

If this is the last light, drown me in memory,
if this is the last meeting in the moment of seeing,
if this is the last of my name from Melanie near-by,
save me from chemistry, drown me in memory.

\*

I count through space, through white noise
scooping out the bowl of language
good science burning my inside out,
good science, they sang in headlong flight.

St. Michael cast down the rebel angels,
every day they dance on Cinquantenaire;
Dr. Otte and Dr. Entezari unlocked the DNA in cells,
every day they dance at the hospital St Pierre.

At night when the chords descend
rinse my heart in wine
skin restraint from my tongue
and let my friends deny death.

## We've brought your husband back to you, the doctor said.

Melanie I don't know how you stood by me,
how you helped make me ready for the surgeon,
shaved me and comforted me and left that evening
driving across the city in a capsule of light.

     Sitting on a collapsed marble column
     outside the room we rented in Naxos town,
     in the heat of the narrow streets of the chora
     looking straight at the camera, a beautiful girl.

How did you attend me as I floated off on the bloody bed?
I am dumb to the bone to say what I must say.
What did you do when I was reduced to flashing numbers?
What did you think in the white pauses of my absence?

     I see you on the ferry to Mull in a red jacket for the rain,
     I don't remember a word, just your face like a light;
     at the rail the sea and sky pitching behind your head,
     the horizon we were crossing over to Mull.

Melanie I don't know how you stood by me,
I was often not there it seems, will you tell me later?
I remember all that you did and all that you brought me
and we were there in that room standing together in flight.

# Afterwards

# To Ian, Recovering

*People here are extraordinarily welcoming. 'Ye are welcome' they say. Feen-none, the name of our house and the village, is a pastoral townland in the middle of highly marginal bog and upland and between the mountains and the sea, referred to as the village.*

Dear Ian

I hope the steady progress continues. I love the picture of Gruff's childhood that you describe. Nine? I thought he was still a toddler, ridiculous of me. The school sounds tuned in – you would know otherwise. What a sweet setting for him, and for you too, on your feet, nearly? It sounds like a distinct world and that it's writing itself for you. Good.

The end of the unrepeatable radiotherapy treatment has been as hard as predicted, nasty but normal, and the good Dr Otte saw me through it. Again I'm humbled by the kindness and skill of the clinicians who have cared for me. I have a big thought – probably on Pinker lines against the pessimistic tide, that we are an astonishing species.

I've tried to explain this to several friends. If I think of everything that has gone into my treatment during this year it is extraordinary – not just the medical expertise, the technology and smart bureaucracy but the sheer human kindness and ethical intention that it is all there and just given. There are thousands of people capable and willing to learn how to do all of this for others who they don't even know.

My amazement doesn't depend on finding out if I'm cured or not. How on earth does this all come about? It is morally extraordinary and we think of it as normal. I am in awe of it. I have been carried high in the arms of *philotomo*, that Greek term. Of course

I do this for you, it is my obligation because we are all people, no? It is my pleasure, it makes us human. You're welcome.

I talked to the nurses at the time of the surgery and haemorrhage. One had just come back from the refugee camps on Lesvos, another was off to the UK to study English Literature because she loved it, and another who wanted to work in ICU all her life. We care for each other, and we're good at it and it astonishes me. To find you're welcome. Enough.

## Below This Level

As of
    today
        PSA
           below
               this
                  level
                      0.
                        01
                           there
                               is
                              none.

## Arrival

At last we came to the first language
birds dropped the carved letters into our hands
calling all night to a pictured childhood,
death was not involved and we were all there.

Every meaning fluttered in the trees,
furled leaves disclosed an original morphology,
graphemes flashed on/off shot through with light
havering around the edge of knowing.

In the lost towns and invisible homelands
jaded clouds tore holes in the account
keeping us apart from our own interest
like slow semantic drift wrong footing thought.

Modes of seeing collapse and are replaced,
nowhere is fixed and the ground is rising up;
only the topographic reveals a sort of truth,
planes tilting around the sleeping houses.

Questions of perception in the village square
restored us step by step to the literal world,
showers of red, blue, white, black, drew the future,
tearing me from the earth that night.

Under such simple conditions
Vitebsk detached my head for dreaming,
we flew out of the bedecked room
X-ray snapped the sky and dissolved the window.

You were always there and I was with you.
Zesty, zesty – said the floating man and left.

# Messages Coming In

Glenn Gould arrived today in the arms of J S Bach
from the garden of morning the aria took flight
over the sun – cracked quay and inclined greenery.
Roger Hilton back flipped a perfect arc – *Get me out of here.*
*Where's my bloody boat and which way is the Côte d'Azur?*

The advocates of Spring dig dig the spreading mulch,
dig the mud, the tubers, the building block sequence
to find the roots of their own ascendency,
at the edge of the turning world silver compounds
proclaiming delight in unlike forms.

Fingers in the soil, at first chthonic cold
rising to blood temperature for us to assume the literal.
I heard the sounds of the world enter all around,
taking shape the solid bodies transduced
by efflorescence, by intelligence into my empty hands.

# Across the Square

Awake this morning to the literal world,
I see Nancy's house across the square in Agios Dimitrios,
dressed in black she hangs a blanket on a rail to air
and there's a freshly painted red box on the wall.

The sea sits on Nancy's left shoulder, light bathes,
and the scene is framed by oleander and a pine tree.
The sparrows and doves are in good voice for the rain
and the clouds stream in banners from the mountain.

I think Nancy's memory has holes in it,
- *You English, did you know my husband George?*
Yes we did, we knew George for eighteen years,
a retired merchant seaman who kept by the sea.

At first he drove the yellow school bus,
he fished in a good sized boat, the Alexandria,
he swam in the harbour and parked by the house after asking;
there's an enamelled picture of his younger face on his gravestone.

For years Nancy pretended to speak no English,
occasionally she sits on her veranda and plays the accordion.
- *Did you know my husband George who was here?*
The sparrows and doves add chorus to her playing.

George's boat is gone, his car is gone, his face is on his gravestone:
to enter the literal world is difficult, falling falling falling.
ο παλιατζής, cries the junk man in his wrecked pick-up,
ο παλιατζής, bring out your used-up things, I'll take them all.

He circles the square, leaves diesel fumes in the trees,
ο παλιατζής ο παλιατζής, Nancy Nancy, play that song.

# Singing with Chagall

Borders of gold
                    studs of silver
I will make
                    a green bed
                                        cedar beams
                                                            fir rafters.

Your banner flies over me
your name fills the sky
my fair one come away.

I will go about the city
the streets and the broadways
and I will find you.

A fountain of gardens
a well of living waters
love is strong as death.

*

Caught in the pink rush of flying fish,
donkeys and goats – did I say that, see that?
Chagall singing up the swoosh of it.

Jerusalem Vitebsk the compass point swings
yellow gazelle blue gazelle a woman in flight
Bathsheba is flying to rest in his arms.

David sings, above his throne he hovers,
I will do a handstand and play the clarino for you,
I will show you a city on a hill and lie with you.

I will paint the darkness green and saturate the sky
and we will live under this canopy just as we choose,
I stray from the text but would not let you go.

The birds fly right side up, it's the world I've inverted,
they sing in single notes suspended to fashion meaning,
ice crystals like coins tossed ringing in the blue.

\*


An unassuming man stands to one side
depicting olive trees, the brimming sea,
playing a fiddle to the drenched sparrows
as everyone comes and goes in the village square.

This morning the leaves have turned electric green,
the day comes rolling down the mountain hot-foot
over grottoes, aquifers, goats and gods;
we could just begin a civilisation here.

It could be Spring in another country transparent
that sweetness, across the stage of the square
the world makes an entrance at the end of waiting,
the fruit and veg man, the junk man, the living and the dead.

She rose up into depthless sky at first light,
cut a forward roll over the mountain and other acrobatics;
neighbours clapped and the children danced,
- *This is the special dance we do to make everything grow.*

A voice from the well explains how it all turns;
hold your nerve birds, auguries are shot.
I'm on all fours, face down to earth's core
to hear the triumph of music in the world.

\*

The sparrows have gathered in the trees
for chaos and their singing contest;
the sun is up, sing you birds of green vertigo.

Between the horizontal and vertical planes
the old woman we thought dead has returned,
she walks in her garden and lights a fire.

The visiting children step down to the shore,
light pours over the mountain at our back
and the sea puts on its cerulean.

Let this be the season of zero gravity
for relocated donkeys and talking myths
for flying fish and Melanie's gaze.

For Asclepios to dance us across the orchestra,
for the Dionysus Transportation Company
to carry us over the stony ground drenched in light.

*Below This Level* is for
my wife Melanie.

With thanks to Dr. Agneessens, Dr. Entezari and Dr. Otte.

The title *Below This Level* is from the song 'Below This Level (Patient's Song)' by Can on the album *Rite Time*; the singer is Malcolm Mooney. References are made to various musicians. Arthur Russell was not a Reverend. 'Get Around To It' is a song by him on *Calling Out of Context*. In 'Oitgang, provisional' the quotation is from *Don Juan*, Canto 1, stanzas 133 and 134. In the third part of *Below This Level* liberal use is made of paintings by Marc Chagall and of memoirs by him and his wife Bella.

www.ingramcontent.com/pod-product-compliance
Lightning Source LLC
Chambersburg PA
CBHW021947040426
42448CB00008B/1277